JOHNNY
A tribute to Love

Jill Luntz

GW00601030

ARTHUR H. STOCKWELL LTD.
Elms Court   Ilfracombe   Devon
Established 1898

© *Jill Luntz, 1994*
First published in Great Britain, 1994

ISBN 0 7223 2851-6

Printed in Great Britain by
Arthur H. Stockwell Ltd.
Elms Court   Ilfracombe
Devon

I dedicate this story to my daughter, Penny, and to my husband, Mike.

To Penny, for the courage she has shown during these dark months following the loss of her most treasured soul mate; her brother.

To Mike, because without him there would be no story to tell.

CONTENTS

Illustrations set between pages 32—33

PROLOGUE

Why do I want to write about my son? Very many reasons crowd my mind.

Maybe because I am so proud of him for what he has achieved in his short life, not only for himself but for the impact he has had on me, my husband Mike, my daughter Penny, and the whole of our family.

Maybe too, how he has influenced the lives of many friends, acquaintances, and relative strangers, simply by being himself.

Maybe, because he had the condition called 'Down's Syndrome' and like a number of other mothers who have written books or newspaper articles about their precious children, I want the world to know that to give birth to a child with extra special needs is not the disaster that one might imagine it to be.

Maybe that reading Johnny's story other Mums and Dads similarly affected can be encouraged and given hope in their troubles.

Maybe, it's because the pain I feel in these early weeks following his death, is eased a little when I think and write of his life.

Maybe because sitting and focusing all my thoughts on him as I write, I feel him close to me, which is so comforting as the void he has left in my heart and my life is so enormous, that at times the overwhelming grief gets the better of me.

Yes all of these reasons are true, but I also want to write about him because his birth, his life, and his death, have been a spiritual experience that has enriched my life tenfold.

He was so full of spontaneous love, gentle friendliness, and sincerity. The kind that contained no hidden innuendoes of ill nature or malevolence of greater or lesser degree that so very often is part of the nature of so many of us. There are moments when I am full of remorse when thinking how my son was taken from me at Christmas — the time of birth and gifts — and in a sense that precious birth and gift of mine has been suddenly snatched away from me by death. As a Christian I believe that his life, now whole and perfect in the company of God his creator, goes on, and these thoughts are those of anguish and sorrow in his loss for myself, Mike and Penny. But the gift that Johnny was and still is, is made more precious by his parting because of the legacy of life's whole meaning that he has left behind.

DEATH

Cars line both sides of the main road, bumper to bumper, and all adjacent roads nearby or leading to St Matthias Church, Torquay, are equally full. "A big funeral today . . . somebody important, a well-known local dignitary, to attract such a crowd . . . .". Passers-by pause and wonder. No, it is not anyone important or particularly well known in the way it was meant. It is my son Johnny who was just fourteen years old, when he died last week.

"Jonathan" the name that means "a gift from God" and oh! what a special gift we have been blessed with. The gift that came in an unexpected and different wrapping, but when accepted and opened, poured out the qualities of love, joy, and radiant purity that was our Johnny.

We will forever thank him for what he has taught us, and for opening so many doors we would never have had the privilege to enter without him.

We give thanks to God our Heavenly Father for allowing us to experience the love of Jesus Christ our Lord, first hand, through our precious son and brother, Johnny.

The date is January 12th 1993, the time 1.30 p.m. and St Matthias Church, Torquay, is full with well over 400 people — family, friends, teachers, doctors, strangers — all present to share in the Thanksgiving Service for the life of our son Johnny. Johnny, who died just seven weeks short of his fifteenth birthday, unexpectedly and suddenly in hospital, after failing to respond to medication, to try to destroy the insidious infection called Bacterial Endocarditis that had penetrated his heart valve and then spread to cause his kidneys to fail.

Johnny was admitted to hospital on Christmas Day, after we had called the duty GP as he wasn't responding to antibiotics at home. We had given it to try to clear a cough that had troubled him for the previous week or two, but which had not made him ill in himself. He had enjoyed the end-of-term excitement at school, fully participating in the Christmas Fayre, the Christmas Dinner, the Christmas Party, (my fourteen-year-old accepting with innocent childish pleasure the gifts from Santa Claus, alias Frank the caretaker), and the Carol Service held at the local Baptist Church.

We had sat, as we had the last eleven years, with all the other proud but moist-eyed parents during the carols, watching Johnny play the drum during the 'Drummer Boy Carol', and taking his part in the service. End of term came and Johnny was excited about the prospect of the holidays.

Christmas Eve saw friends coming for drinks and mince pies, with Johnny pleased as ever to entertain folk. He was such a sociable gregarious child. Cousins Wendy and Sara arrived to stay over the Christmas period with us. The sense of wonder, in the anticipation of Father Christmas coming that night. The preparation of the letters written with his sister's help, and the careful placing of the pillowcases on the landing, all promised our fourteenth experience of Christmas joy with our darling son.

On Christmas morning Johnny went through the motions of opening his gifts, sitting in bed with my husband and I, but it was obvious he was feeling unwell. He fiercely resisted his illness, and tackled the presents under the tree with the kind of determination to overcome all, that he had shown throughout his life when coughs, colds and infections had troubled or set him back. After this he seemed to tire so, and I found him fast asleep at the top of the stairs. When he woke he burst into tears with the spasmodic pains gripping his tummy, which had swollen considerably. After the duty doctor's second call out, he was admitted to Torbay Hospital through Casualty. X-rays were taken which showed a pneumonia; an intravenous drip was attached and he was taken to the Children's Ward. I stayed the night with him, and Mike returned home to Penny, Wendy and Sara. This began our twelve-day struggle with him and for him, which tragically ended his life here on earth.

Johnny's courage and spirit in hospital during those twelve days was an inspiration to us and to everybody who visited, nursed or treated him. I know I would have been fearful and full of complaints about the necessary treatment to which he was subjected. He never once objected or cried. He watched the procedures asking questions, having a conversation, or sharing a joke with the staff as they prodded or probed. The strong character and undaunted spirit which he had shown throughout his life, remained with him to the end.

BIRTH, LIFE AND LOVE

There are two certain things that we can be sure will happen to us in our humanity. One is birth and the other is death. This is the story of the birth and the death of my son Jonathan, and how the grief I felt at both his birth and his death, was transformed to become the love and life of both earth and heaven.

My baby was born at 4.20 p.m., one Monday afternoon in February: the twenty-seventh day in 1978. "It's a boy!" The midwife showed him to me briefly and then to Mike, my husband, before taking him to the other side of the delivery room and giving him oxygen. He certainly looked a funny blue-grey colour, very different to my daughter's rosy hue after her birth.

During the morning that day I had prepared and popped a chicken into the oven to roast for lunch, and had seen to the needs of my fifteen-month-old daughter Penelope. Leaving her with Mike, I drove the three miles to Paignton to shop. I was aware of some cramp-like aches in my tummy, but put it down to digestive troubles, as my second child was not due for another fortnight. I recall I carried very heavy bags of groceries from the supermarket to the car, and feeling satisfied with my lot, I returned home.

In the meantime Mike had completed the cooking, and we were able to sit down to our lunch straight away. Mike had been a bachelor of forty-four years when we married two years earlier, and was a very accomplished cook. (He proposed to me over a magnificent dish of home-roasted pheasant!) As we ate and chatted over how fortunate we were, the gorgeous little daughter we had, and soon to be blessed with a second child, the pains seemed to be more regular and more pronounced. After timing the intervals between each period of discomfort, I suspected it could well be the first stage of labour after all!

After a quick telephone call to my parents asking them to meet us at our GP's surgery, we drove across town to keep the appointment for Penny's third and final vaccination in infancy; I was determined I was going to be with her for this. By now the pains were coming stronger and at regular intervals, and as the practice nurse taking the Baby Clinic was a midwife, I asked her to check me. "Get yourself to the hospital at once!" was her immediate response.

Mike drove me to Torbay Hospital where I was admitted to the Mary Delve Maternity Ward, and Penny went home in the loving care of her nana and grandad. After a brief examination and a shot of Pethidine in my leg, Johnny arrived just an hour and a half later, after what had been a very short but perfect labour and delivery, weighing in at 8lbs 5ozs.

My pregnancy had been wonderfully happy, carefree, and without hiccups; I had seen a scan of my baby at around sixteen weeks, and all appeared to be perfect. My questions about the possibility of problems because of my age, were answered with positive assurance that problems were most unlikely to occur and that I shouldn't worry. The birth was an exhilarating experience unlike Penny's, where the labour had lasted all night, and in the end I had had a forceps delivery, and my husband had been sent out of the room. Mike had been able to share in the birth of his son with me, and I was so glad of that.

Despair, horror, a deep-seated feeling of anguish, and bitter disappointment welled up inside me when I looked at my son. "A mongol. Oh please God not a mongol. It's not a mongol is it?" was all I could think. Not, he's a mongol, but 'It's' a mongol as if I was looking at some kind of subhuman monster. I was certain it was so, even though no-one had actually said so. (Thankfully that ghastly term mongol has been dropped, and these gentle fun-loving people who have been so cruelly labelled in the past, should now live their lives proudly as they justly deserve. The stigma that that label conjured up needs to be buried for ever.) I said nothing of my fears then but just accepted the midwife's reassurances that my son was fine, except that he was cold and shivering and needed to be put into an incubator for warmth. An 8lb 5oz baby put into an incubator and nothing was wrong, I just couldn't believe her. "Do you think he looks all right?" I asked Mike. He didn't think there was any cause for concern so I said nothing more then. After precious moments together, Mike left to return home to tell the family the good news; a baby boy; a brother for Penny, the perfect family.

Later in the ward, with my baby's incubator beside my bed, I lay there, my mind in turmoil. Everything about him as I gazed into that incubator indicated that my fears were real. The shape of his head with the very high forehead — but, NO that was just a family likeness; my critical eyes crept from the top of his dear little head to the bottom of his toes, mentally noting the low set ears with their flipped over tops, the flattened bridge of his nose, his funny star-shaped hands and the unusual crease lines on the bottom of his feet; the little tip of his tongue between his lips that were open. Perhaps these considerations are not forefront in the thoughts of the average new Mum, but I kept remembering the Down's Syndrome child I had once had in a past teaching post. As I was an 'Elderly Primate' as the gynaecologist had so poetically described me early in my pregnancy, and I was approaching my thirty-seventh birthday! I was, I suppose more aware therefore that the risks of abnormalities were greater.

Mike returned later with Penny and Nana and Grandad. How I treasure the memory of my baby girl running up through the middle of the ward on her little legs, (she'd not long been walking) to greet me, laughing and shouting "Mummy" at the top of her voice and her mop of fair ringlets dancing under their ribbons. As her brother was still in his incubator and being unable to touch or hold him, she couldn't really identify with this small baby. I recall a worried expression on my mother's face and of her not saying too much. Because I was feeling rather tired by now, they all left me to sleep; and later in the evening Mike returned. Even then he was not at all worried and I tried to love my baby as much as he did. The incubator was taken into the Nursery for the night. When I was encouraged to go and feed my baby in the early hours, I expressed my fears to the nurse on duty. She said she didn't know, but would mention to the Senior Staff that I was anxious. I had put the nurses on the spot by asking such questions, as they are not in a position to give answers or information until the doctors have done so. Much later when in conversation with them, they had told me how difficult it had been for them emotionally and professionally.

During the afternoon of the following day when doing his ward rounds, the Consultant Paediatrician called us into his office. He began by saying "I hear you are worried about your baby" — and I so vividly remember the details of the next twenty minutes. It was I who first mentioned the word 'mongol' and not he — and I was told afterwards that frequently mothers receiving bad news of their baby's condition, bear a grudge against the bearer of that bad news — I give full marks to the skilful way in which he handled our distress, and the very real care that he showed towards us. He said that the term 'mongol' was not used and the condition was 'Down's Syndrome' so these babies were called Down's babies. Down's Syndrome so called after the doctor who discovered that the underlying cause was due to an extra chromosome to the normal forty-six. In man, every cell of the body has forty-six chromosomes arranged in twenty-three matching pairs. If for any reason, there is more or less chromosome material, a disorder in growth and development is likely to occur. Down's Syndrome children have forty-seven chromosomes. He stressed he needed a blood test to confirm his suspicions, but he felt fairly certain that our baby did in fact have Down's Syndrome.

We stayed in that office for what seemed like hours, hugging each other and sobbing and trying to make sense of the devastation we were feeling. Mike was far more rational than I, quite simply stating "This is my son. I love him. So what, that he has this label? It doesn't change a thing as far as I am concerned."

For the remainder of that week in hospital I was given a room to myself. The hours that I stood looking into that cradle and feeling no love for my baby. I felt nothing but pity for him and a terrible sense of guilt. I felt I had consciously inflicted this dreadful handicap on this morsel of humanity. For hours I sobbed; a waterfall plunging into the seemingly bottomless pit of despair. A waterfall of self-pity. Why should such a thing have happened to me? These tears were also a form of bereavement too — I had lost the normal baby I thought I was having and this was a second-best replacement. How could I possibly take this child home? He would ruin all the happiness in my marriage; the burden he would bring would destroy everything for me. He wasn't perfect — I had always been a perfectionist. I wished he would die. I didn't love him. I didn't want him. How could God do such a thing to me?

Normal reactions the experts would say. I have many friends, other Mums of Down's children, or children with different special needs, who felt similarly affected in the early days, weeks and months. Thank goodness for their contact and friendship. We have all given one another the kind of special support that only those who have experienced the same anguish can give. I regret that I wasn't part of a Church fellowship at this time, as I now know and value the love and the prayers of our extended family — the Church; in our case the Anglican Church of St Matthias in Torquay.

It was such a strange thing that when the news of our baby circulated through our local community, so many felt it inappropriate to send us cards. Having had about 150 after Penny's birth, it was an added heartbreak to receive so few. It was of course that folk simply did not know what to say. Did they congratulate or commiserate. Attitudes have greatly changed for the better now, thankfully, and I would be surprised to hear the same reactions these days.

I had had some counselling from doctors and nurses alike, all trying to help me through that difficult first week. The nurses were great in the pains they took to encourage a bonding between my baby and me; I continued to show reluctance to accept him. "Why me?" consumed me. "Why not you?" was the retort received from a very wise Health

Visitor, during her home visit to me later on. Oh yes I could legally walk out of that hospital and refuse to take my baby with me: he could then be fostered. I considered this option quite seriously. Of course the family bond being full of great strength and love, helped to push these negative thoughts aside and I walked to the car carrying my son in my arms one week after his birth.

Johnny was such a good baby with a placid disposition. He rarely cried in the early weeks, just making a faint little squeak from time to time. I feel overwhelming love and longing for my child as I remember those evenings in the first month, spent walking back and forth the length of our lounge: Mike and I in turn cradling him to relieve the spasmodic pains of colic whilst the exquisite duet from Bizet's Opera "The Pearl Fishers" filled the room; its soothing effect bringing peace and calm to both Johnny and us! He slept soundly until his next feed. I recall the enormous effort it took for Johnny to take his feeds. Sucking made him so breathless. At the time I didn't think it could be anything other than his physical weakness. He, like all Down's babies resembled a rag doll to handle; his arms and legs flopping without much control due to poor muscle development. He was loose-ligamented or double-jointed, and when lying on his back his body could be likened to that of a dead chicken with legs splayed. Later on when he was much older, he delighted in showing us how easily he could do the 'splits' and twist himself into shapes and positions from super-advanced yoga!

He was an angelic little soul to look at, with cherub lips and a fine dusting of sandy red hair; and the first month at home passed with much the same routine as for any other new baby. He was troubled by a chest infection at six weeks, and was admitted into hospital with pneumonia. It was at this time that a heart murmur was detected, but we were given no indication of its severity at this stage. Antibiotics had the desired effect and we returned home. Three weeks later we were back in the ward, this time with a severe bout of bronchitis. After discussions with the paediatrician, Johnny was transported by ambulance to The Bristol Children's Hospital. So began our liaison with the Cardiac Team. This was the beginning of almost fifteen years of regular Consultations, Chest X-rays, ECGs, fun with the nurses in the Outpatients and a good rapport and respect for the Cardiac Specialist.

A two-week stay in Bristol, and exploratory Catheterisation Surgery determined the extent and severity of the abnormality in Johnny's heart. He had an AV Canal Defect, which in lay terms meant a large hole in the centre of his heart, and all four chambers open to the free flow of blood, and also there was a defective valve.

Now after three months had passed, a strong love bond had developed between me and my special baby. It seemed such a cruel blow when we learnt that medically there was little hope of his survival beyond his first birthday. "Please God let him die now" was all I could think. The longer we cared for him the greater the ultimate heartbreak, kept flashing through my mind. "Please spare us that" I inwardly pleaded. Full of even deeper grief and despair we returned home with our bottles of Digoxin (the heart drug) and Lasix (the anti-fluid retention drug).

We lived on what seemed like a permanent knife edge at first, not daring to breathe over him for fear of giving him some kind of infection. This state of affairs could not continue, and so after the initial pain of confusion came acceptance, and the realism that each and everyone of us in the family must take his chance to live as normal a life as possible, and that included Johnny. His first year and subsequent early life was one of repeated infections and almost permanent antibiotics; as he grew, we could see even in his infancy, that strength and determined character showing through. He fought off every infection — with the help of modern medicine, and I accept, careful nurturing on our part; his first birthday passed by. "We are so sorry, it is very unlikely he will survive two years" was the medical opinion, as the abnormal forceful free flow of blood within his heart was stressful to the whole system, and as he grew and became more active so the added strain would take its toll.

He showed blueness around his lips, fingers and toes, generally only when he had an infection. From the chest

X-rays it was apparent that his lungs were under considerable strain, and pulmonary hypertension developed and steadily worsened throughout his life. However Johnny seemed so strong physically, even when his activity levels developed as he got older, and it was difficult to realise how major his problem was just by looking at him. He enjoyed his exercise sessions lying on the rug, with all of us taking turns to lift his arms and legs, bending and stretching them repeatedly to strengthen his muscle tone. At three months he smiled — that wonderful experience doubly intensified in his case — at five months those squeals of delight when his sister came near, and the fun between these two babies of mine (Penny was still only twenty months) brought sheets of tears washing my face. Now they were tears of a kind of joy and happiness of such intensity I could never have imagined, when those tears of self-pity flowed in the hospital after his birth.

After a failed childless first marriage, and up to three years living in the Far East, two in East Africa and three in the Middle East in Beirut, where I had been working and living a life of abundance in terms of materialism, travel and glamour, I had built an invisible shield around my emotional self, fearful of another hurtful relationship. I look back on this period in my life as a valuable part of my own personal tapestry, one of opportunities grasped firmly and valuable lessons learnt, and great memories and long-lasting friendships made. I feel grateful, but life took on a new meaning in those early months of Johnny's life. LOVE took over my life from these moments on. Lady Luck played her part in Mike and I finding one another. He was forty-four and I thirty-five when we married. He is a man with such an abundance of love that flows without restraint, and I regret the times I have hurt him (albeit unintentionally) by my own selfishness, and my inability to demonstrate tactile affection as readily and as unrestrainedly as he. Grateful love and wonder at the miracle of birth when our precious daughter was born. She was so perfect a baby, contented and of a sunny and smiling disposition when strangers 'oohed' and 'aahed' over her pram! The temporary period after Johnny's birth, when I looked LOVE in the face but was blind to it, was so short that it was merely a hiccup in what has been a wonderful fifteen-year period in my life.

I don't pretend that life bringing up two children with only fifteen months between them at our ages, has been plain sailing. We have had our share of irritation and frustration, disturbed and frequent sleepless nights with worry over Johnny's health. The additional care that Johnny needed, the long period before he walked, took its toll on, among other things, my back, with the never-ending bending, picking up and carrying of a rather solid little chap. The inevitable friction between us at times, due to the pressures of our individual daily lives; the stress of Mike's work involving great responsibility and skill; our strong characters, both having our own ideas and the fact that we were single for so long and making our own decisions, my busy daily routine and not sufficient sleep, caused minor tiffs. But then that is life in the raw within a personal relationship one with another, and I guess most of us experience these moments. But with love and a sense of commitment they become trivial and are easily overthrown. Love is the conqueror.

When Johnny came home from Bristol Children's Hospital at three months, we decided to have a portrait photograph taken professionally. The prognosis was so poor for Johnny's health we thought we wouldn't have him for long. It's a beautiful photograph, Johnny is gazing up into his sister's face and she is bending to give him a kiss. Penny was then just eighteen months old.

During his first year we had many visitors all intent on his and our wellbeing. The Heath Visitors, Social Workers, Pre-School Advisory Teachers in Special Education being the main professionals. They all brought words of wisdom and sound advice. On bodily health there was exercise regimes to do regularly at home, visits to the Cardiac Clinic every three months, the Eye Clinic for inspection and patches for a lazy eye, the GP's Surgery for doses of antibiotics and physiotherapy for his persistent coughs and colds and chest infections, endless different creams to try and clear unexplained rashes, chapped split lips and cheeks, and sore bottom! On mental health and intellect, the pre-school teacher brought toys and ideas for stimulation techniques. We rigged up mobiles everywhere Johnny happened to be positioned! He loved two posts with a washing line strung between them and weird and wonderful objects hanging just within reach to touch, push or kick, so encouraging him to investigate and learn. All of these sensory experiences were so vital for him, but Penny was his most vital learning tool. She played by him and with him, he learning from her every move and communication. The laughter and fun they shared, the love and companionship they had together, brought joy to us.

As a small baby, Johnny spent his waking hours sitting in his bouncy chair either near Penny or me, where we were able to constantly stimulate him by talking, singing, touching and playing with him. He was able to press himself up on his hands, holding his head steady, at four to five months, and started creeping on his tummy, rolling over and then trying to crawl at six and a half months. At seven months he managed to sit up from a cradled position. He was travelling across the floor by rolling over and over at eight and a half months, and sitting steadily without support at ten months. It was at this time that I regularly sat him on a potty, and from then on we never had a soiled nappy, which I thought a tremendous achievement. He was up on his hands and knees in a crawling position trying, but not actually managing to move. He was still at this stage when he had his first birthday. He was in fact eighteen months old when he finally crawled, but still only on elbows and knees. He enjoyed standing and walking a few steps when both hands were held, from eighteen months onwards.

This was the beginning of my back-breaking period which seemed endless. Looking back at these early records of achievement, it is interesting to note the pattern of learning which seems to be typical in Down's Syndrome. These patterns continued throughout his life in mental and physical development. He had spurts of great progress and then a period when he 'plateaued', not showing any further advancement for several months at a time. He was two years old before he was able to pull himself up into a standing position and take a few steps unaided but holding on to the furniture. This did not prevent him getting from A to B though, he was very adept at bouncing along on his bottom, and indeed covering a considerable distance if the motivation was there.

As with all toddlers, even non-walkers, I needed eyes in the back of my head, as among other things the stairs were a great attraction and he could easily crawl up these! It was not until just before his fourth birthday that he walked unaided. Having had an extension built on to the side of our house, we were able to use the area leading directly from the kitchen as a playroom. This was invaluable as I was able to see and play with Penny and Johnny and do my chores at the same time. We built a worktop all along one wall with shelving underneath for all the toys, at a low enough level for a non-walker to reach with ease; the teacher in me coming out again!

Sitting on the carpet surrounded by bricks delicately balanced into castles, or colourful giant triangular walls soon to be dashed and scattered accompanied by gleeful chuckles and guffaws, and then gentle remonstrating from Penny, "Oh Johnny look what you've gone and done now!" Suddenly and without forethought as far as I could tell, Johnny stood up amidst the mess and walked across the room to me. It was an electrifying moment. In total disbelief I clasped him in my arms "Oh Johnny. Oh Johnny. Oh Johnny. You walked, you walked all by yourself . . . I can't believe it!" Penny looked bemused and not wanting to be done out of a cuddle joined us, and with my arms wrapped tightly around them both, there I was crying buckets again.

Although the first steps had been taken, these gross motor movements developed slowly over the next few years, so there was little respite for my aching back muscles. We persevered with all the training activities that encouraged the continual development of the gross and fine motor movements, emphasising co-ordination between all these physical things and realising the vital link between the mental and the physical.

In all of his life Johnny, even from these small baby beginnings, like getting eye contact, that first smile, the first word or gesture of communication, to the end of his life showed an insatiable appetite for knowledge. He was never one to just sit and gaze vacantly into space. Among the very few occasions when he showed such tendencies was when he came home after a full day at school, and like the rest of us 'switched off' as a form of relaxation from an exciting and physically and mentally exacting day's work.

But after what seemed to us to be such a short space of time, especially when he was older, there he was pestering for more attention. Seeking knowledge through his early play activities, and then through the years the more advanced board games, colouring and drawing, and writing games, his school reading books, "I'm just doing my homework Mum" — his story books from his bedroom library, his game of darts that had to be exactly modelled on the TV game of 'Bull's-eye' positioning ourselves as the contestants did, and most importantly imitating the voice of the presenter, are but a few of the examples of what he enjoyed. Poor Mike constantly dragged from his chair to play a form of hockey, basketball, football, hopscotch and the ever popular games of 'What's the time Mr Wolf?' and 'Please Mr Crocodile, may I cross the water?'

The scene is Mike sitting at his desk in his study, desk top strewn with papers, and Mike in deep concentration. Johnny silently pads across the kitchen, *en route* for the study. It could almost be a shadow standing there outside the open door, motionless for a spell then the slight twist of the head and a heaving sigh. Another sigh. No response. Hugely exaggerated heavy breathing. "Dad . . ." "Yes darling . . ?" "I'm bored." "Well why not go and play with your games or watch a video?" "Will you play with me?" "Sorry love, I'm really very busy" . . . . . more enormous sighs. "Please?" "No." "Please?" "No." "PLeeeese?" "NO." Johnny retreats with a look of utter rejection, only to reappear within seconds fully dressed in anorak, hat, gloves and woolly scarf, and outdoor shoes, dragging Mike's heavy waxed jacket, woolly hat and gloves. "I've got a good idea Dad. Let's play hockey on the patio!" I'm not at all surprised to see Johnny leading Mike by the hand, who is now fully geared up for the cold east wind outside, with a triumphant grin from ear to ear. Before long I hear the excitement and loud chatter from one happy boy and his best pal, as they enjoy themselves as best mates can!

Yes it got a bit wearing to say the least in the latter days, as we advanced in years, and unlike Johnny who was all 'get up and go' we often resented the intrusion upon our need to just sit and relax. But his powers of persuasion, using his considerable charm to its best advantage, and so cunningly executed, never failed to rouse, particularly his Daddy's instincts of loving tenderness and willingness to please. I often made the excuse of domestic chores needing to be done, and although Johnny helped me dry the dishes, bake, vacuum the floor and iron simple items, these spurts of domesticity on his part, were only when it suited him!

I also felt very strongly that even from the earliest years we all had a rightful position, equally important within the family. It would have been very easy to have lived our daily lives around Johnny's needs as he required so much extra attention, but Penny's requirements were of equal importance, and our needs too had to be met. We tried to instill this into Johnny's learning from babyhood. I have seen how very difficult this can be with a child needing additional care within a family framework, and how the pressures can cause emotional damage to other siblings, and the breakdown of a marriage. We just did what we believed to be the best for our family situation, trying to work together as a team of four, having our disagreements from time to time certainly, but somehow resolving them, and thank God it generally worked out over the years.

Shortly after Johnny's birth I was introduced to a group of mothers whose children were then around five years old. They had not had the advantages that we had had, following their babies' births, and had formed a self-help group locally. They initiated their action as they were disappointed and felt let down by the inadequate and inappropriate support that was available to them at that time from both the areas of Health and Education. A very positive post of "Pre-School Advisory Teacher" had emerged from the Education Office. Their liaisons with her, the Social Services Department, and the Health Department, developed and continued to improve positively over the years. They were a strong band who fought for the rights of their children, and found solace in, and support for one another in every activity in which they found themselves engaged.

We have all remained firm friends, standing alongside each other in all the difficulties we have faced over the years. These difficulties ranged from lack of necessary nursery and playschool provisions, to actually setting up the very successful "Opportunity Playgroup" for pre-school children with special needs, from joining together in the highly beneficial 'Toy Library' sessions, and sharing cups of coffee and airing our grievances as the local branch of the 'Down's Syndrome Association' got under way. Links for me later with Mayfield Special School, long before Johnny began his formal education there, were through the headmistress, formerly the Pre-School Advisory Teacher, and this band of dynamic mums, who continued to work so hard for the benefit of their children.

They gave great encouragement to new mums like me. One of these mums came with her husband to see Mike and me when Johnny was just a few months old, to exchange not only the real and meaningful tales of confused emotions and feelings after their baby son was born, but to share also the positive attitudes of looking forward with hope, and the delight they were now experiencing as they watched the progress of their Down's son. That and many other "get-togethers" were all very encouraging and helped to lift the pessimism which set in from time to time. Another dear friend, who experienced the heartbreak of losing her son as a baby and then having fostered a little Down's girl lost her also as a baby, went on to adopt a baby boy, and the joy she continues to experience as her Down's son is now approaching his teens, warms our heart. She has been such an inspiration to so many of us. Later on Mike and I went on to become the 'liaison' parents, our job being to visit new parents of Down's Babies in this area, but only when parents requested this link via the hospital or their GP. We were able to pass on our experiences and so continue the back-up support alongside the professionals. We were just an ordinary family like those we were helping, the difference being that we had actually shared their feelings first-hand, and consequently were able to truly relate.

After the Opportunity Group came into being, and from

when Johnny was about eighteen months old, we started attending the two mornings they met each week, in the local Health Clinic in Paignton. The physiotherapist who was responsible for the daily management, and other kindly volunteers, gave up their time willingly to care for up to ten children with both mental and physical disabilities, all of whom were under five years of age. A group of friends from my area, all mums with their own busy daily schedules, gave up their time willingly to join in a rota of car drivers, to transport the children to and from their homes. I stayed with Johnny to begin with, and Penny was able to enjoy the activities and games as much as he. When it was obvious that Johnny could be left happily engaged and stimulated, with peace of mind I left and enjoyed the unaccustomed pleasure of just Penny's company; she and I spending a few pleasant hours together feeding the ducks in the park or shopping and me able to give her my undivided attention.

This was a very vital facility for not only the disabled child, who enjoyed the obvious advantages of stimulation through well-designed play activities and having individual milestones monitored and recorded, but also for the parents, especially the mothers, to have a few well-earned and deserved hours' break. The group was of great benefit to all, and in particular through social interaction, where the disability of any child made communication extremely difficult. Cheers resounded each time any little one in that group achieved a new goal, especially if it was getting eye contact where there had previously been none, a first smile or grasp of a hand, sitting up unaided, a crawl or a shaky step forward.

The children were referred to the Opportunity Playgroup by the Health Service, and came any time from a year of age, which is a much younger admission than at a normal playgroup. This afforded the children a much longer stay where they could be encouraged to achieve their maximum potential, particularly in areas of toilet training and feeding before they began education after their fifth birthday. Very many of the children went on to enjoy activities in their local playgroups wherever possible. Johnny joined his sister at her playgroup when he was three, having spent a very rewarding eighteen months at the Opportunity Group. This group continues to thrive under new leadership, and over the years has gone from strength to strength. With financial help coming their way in charitable donations from local organisations like the Lions Club, among others, to which Mike belonged, they have been able to purchase and run their own minibus for many years now.

So life settled to routine through the baby stage and into the toddler stage. The regular visits from the Pre-School Teacher was a lovely contact, and we followed her advice on how to get the best out of Johnny. We marked off his achievements when he reached his goals, on the Portage Scheme. The Portage Scheme is a check list divided into all the areas of learning from birth, through the baby milestones in Infant Stimulation, Self-Help, Socialisation, Language, Motor and Cognitive Skills. As an ex-teacher I tended to be a bit too preoccupied by placing emphasis on the learning skills, and forgot that learning takes place equally well within the framework of the everyday home situations. So it was quite a struggle at times to balance out my priorities, and keep everything in proper perspective; and trying too hard to overcompensate when one's child is mentally impaired, leads to even greater stress.

Within the normal every day-to-day routine in the home, Johnny's disability didn't make too great an impact on me. It always hit me face on when out mixing with friends who had several ordinary children, or when in the company of all the other handicapped children. I loved him, but it was at least two years before I fully accepted Johnny intellectually, as the unique individual that he was. Why did I place so much emphasis and importance on intelligence? I know that subconsciously he was still a big disappointment, he had thrown my ideas of 'perfection' and pierced my sense of pride. Thinking back to these early years and remembering these confused emotions, I am so grateful to him for putting the record straight. As one mother wrote:

"Take ego away from parental love and what flowers is more passion than I ever thought possible. And not everyday love but a superior version, because the selfish element is cut to the bone."

Johnny's sunny nature was a redeeming feature and taught me that creating love is simple. He was such an amenable child and so co-operative; I can truthfully say he never showed any traits of bad temper or spite in normal childish ways. He was easy going, and when he wanted something his sister had, he somehow managed to achieve his aim without causing a quarrel. Had his inborn nature been different, I can't say how I might have reacted. I had a lot to learn about human expectation.

It was apparent on the medical side that he needed corrective treatment for a squint. We made visits to the Ophthalmology Department at the hospital, and patches were prescribed for his lazy eye, to be applied for an hour a day. Our frequent visits to the Cardiologist continued. We joined in the Speech Therapy Clinic too, and Johnny lived through these early years, bouncing back continually from chest infections. He was practically permanently on antibiotics. He wasn't the easiest baby to feed. Mainly because of the effort it took to drink his milk, and his solid food was liquidised for far longer a period of time than usual, as he gagged on lumps, and his teeth were so slow in coming through. Then when he was the proud owner of a few teeth to enable him to chew, he began the awful habit of grinding! He ground his front milk teeth right down to the gums, so biting on anything hard was impossible.

When he was about three and a half years old, he had a severe bout of bronchitis and became dehydrated. At this stage the main problem was encouraging him to take in enough fluids — you can take a horse to water, but you can't make him drink — took on a new meaning to me. I was exasperated! Johnny flatly refused to drink no matter how hard we tried to make a game of it. He became very listless and was admitted to the hospital with severe dehydration and acute heart failure. If he had not been in the oxygen tent in the ward when his heart showed considerable stress, we might well have lost him then. It was a worrying spell but Johnny bounced back smiling.

It was around this time that we started attending morning service at St Matthias Church, Wellswood, Torquay; the Reverend Canon Peter Larkin was the Rector. Changes had been made to encourage families with young children and a crèche facility was available for the very youngest children. It enabled us to go and enjoy the services without constantly fretting about the children disturbing the older members of the congregation. We were so very grateful when Revd Larkin came to see Johnny in hospital, and the prayers at his bedside were very moving. Until now I had been a "loose" sort of Christian, going for the 'Special Festivals', and not really thinking much about why I was there, and now I felt a real desire to hear and learn more about Christianity, and deepen my own faith and grow in the knowledge of God's role in my life.

Johnny and Penny loved going to St Matthias Church, and joined in with their friends regularly in the Sunday Children's Groups. Johnny started in the crèche, graduated to the Scramblers (three to four year olds), the Climbers (five to six year olds) and then the Explorers. He participated fully in all the activities with a little help from his friends. A good number of the mums helped in the running of the groups, and I did my share too. Johnny loved to join the other children out front during the services, singing and miming to specially loved hymns and short sketches; he played various parts over the years in the children's events for Christmas, Easter or the other special events in the Christian calendar, and gained so much in confidence and maturity. He retained all the facts from the Bible stories, and he and we gained in the sure knowledge of God's love. He was a hit with the elderly folk with his spontaneous love and I know they revelled in his welcome as he handed out the hymn books with a hug and a cuddle thrown in for good measure! After a long spell helping in the groups, the responsibility became a strain, as there was preparation required and meetings to attend, and on top of all there was to do with my family, I was relieved to hand over to a successor!

After his latest spell in hospital, it was suggested that we go again to the Children's Hospital in Bristol for more cardiac investigations. A second catheterisation test showed no change in the deformity in his heart, but there was increased hypertension in his lungs, due to the abnormal malfunction of his heart. It was decided that even if surgery were attempted it could not give him any promise of improvement or even survival on the operating table. We had to accept that surgery was not an option we could consider, and that we would just carry on as we had done so far with drug therapy, regular check-ups and faith in God's will.

By now Johnny had started joining in the fun at the Woodlands Playgroup. As he was still very unsure walking unaided, I was concerned about his general welfare, knowing full well that Wendy, and her lady helpers had all they could cope with, caring for the safety of the lively three to five year olds attending. We were able to secure the one-to-one help of a lovely lady called Connie, after discussions and liaisons with the Education and Health Departments. My mind was at rest when I left him two, and later three mornings a week under her safe supervision. He crossed several major milestones during his time there. He joined wearing a nappy, but discarded it very swiftly, wanting to and learning to use the toilets like the other children. Crawling in preference to walking, but soon realising his disadvantages at such a low level, he became much more adept and confident on his feet. His time there overlapped with his sister, but she left to begin Primary School a year after he had started. Johnny was very popular with the other children, and it warmed my heart and tears pricked my eyes when I watched their reactions towards him.

It was now decision time regarding his choice of schooling. We were very tempted to send him along to Ilsham Primary School with Penny, as the headmaster was very keen that he should go. Gordon, who had had experience with older Down's students in Zimbabwe on an overseas job, and he was rather biased towards Johnny as he was his Godfather, very much wanted him there. After very much discussion and visiting our local 'special school' just three miles from where we lived, we decided Mayfield School was the right choice. At this time there was not so much pressure on parents to consider mainstream placements. I can only speak from my own experience but I do not regret the choice Mike and I made for Johnny.

Mayfield School has a wonderfully positive, caring and happy atmosphere. We felt it immediately. There was an air of commitment and love; laughter and fun went hand in hand with concentrated carefully-structured learning, from the first days in the Nursery to the latter days in the Leavers. Avis, our very dear friend the headmistress when Johnny began his education there, was responsible for making this school into the place of excellence that it has become. She was blessed with a natural ability, and her commitment to the school has gained our respect and gratitude. Of course a captain cannot sail the ship single-handed, and her crew of men and women teachers, and classroom assistants, supported her ideals and put the theories into practice. Children at this school made strides and were encouraged to reach their potential all along the line — music and dancing, arts and crafts, PE and sports, the 3Rs, cooking, shopping, visits to town, outings arranged to incorporate a learning skill of some kind. Special visitors to the school bringing the outside world in. Theatre group workshops, professional musicians, and art and craft specialists all added to the pageantry of this school's provision for the benefit of our children.

Johnny began his time in the Nursery Class with Shirley, whom he adored, and his love for her continued as he moved through the classes. He attended mornings only sessions the term before his fifth birthday, and combined these with his visits to the Woodlands Playschool during that first term. The best of both worlds suited him, with the familiarity of playschool linking in with the initiation into 'proper school', so easing him into a gradual acceptance of life without Mum away from home. This didn't pose any real problem because of Johnny's natural sociability and adaptation.

We had been encouraged from the very earliest years to accustom him to being without us. This was exceedingly painful when we accepted we needed a holiday without him. He was just ten months old when we spent two weeks in Rhodes, leaving him in the John Parks Unit of Torbay Hospital. This is a unit for long and short-term care for the profoundly disabled young children. The holiday was wonderful, but the homecoming and being reunited with our precious baby was even more so. We left him again the following year in the same way. Yes, we needed a holiday, and yes it was just as much a wrench to make the decision a second time. The fact that he was in the "hospital", was reassuring in a medical sense, but I fretted about the institutional aspect of it. Not long after this, Devon Social Services began the excellent Family Relief Scheme. Volunteer host families taking in our disabled youngsters on a daily or longer basis, were recruited to provide relief for the families. For us it was heaven sent; the pairing up of the two families was carefully thought out and training sessions were held. Jane and Merv, and their two children Paula and Darren, were a great source of comfort to us and a second home for Johnny. He loved being with them, playing with the children, taken on exciting outings and being thoroughly spoilt; I never worried about leaving him in their care. Holidays were taken without him again the following year, when Johnny was still only three and I could not risk taking him out of the country because of his continuing infections, and anyway it was the complete break and physical rest that I needed so badly.

We were lucky to have had the Family Relief Scheme throughout Johnny's life. Jane and Merv were unable to continue offering hospitality after several years, and after a period without help, our dear friends Ann and Tom offered themselves. Johnny continued to go to them over a period of many years, sometimes just for an afternoon or overnight stay, or for longer spells if it was unsuitable for him to come with us. Ann was a classroom assistant at school, so Johnny knew her well, and we will be forever grateful for the love and care she, Tom and their family showed him. Nothing was too much trouble. She encouraged his participation in domestic chores and achieved far more than I ever did! She took him on visits and excursions all around the area, and he did "manly" things with Uncle Tom; he always came home with his diary written up, and it was great to read it with him and have a means of talking through his experiences with him.

Around the time of puberty, we noticed some reluctance on his part to leave us as readily as before. But with gentle persuasion and giving clear explanations as to the reasons why he couldn't be with us, we left him. Although outwardly it might not have been apparent, I believe he pined a little inside. We made timetables for him to tick off the days, and with his daily diary he was able to understand the element of time a little. We sent lots of postcards, and spoke to him on

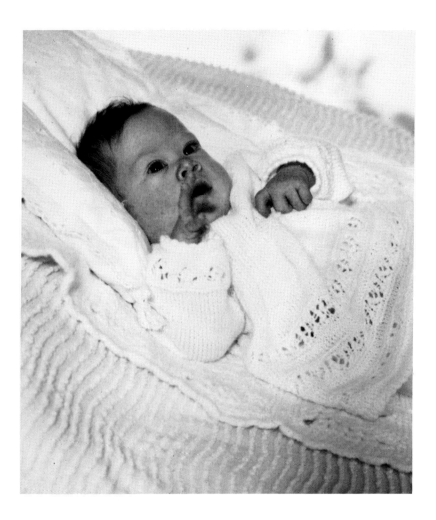

*"We are so sorry to tell you it is very unlikely
that your son will see his first birthday"*

Happy Birthday
One Year Old Today

And so the learning processes begin . . . .

*A little mouse in
the School Panto
"Cinderella"*

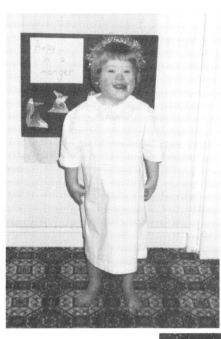

Nativity Plays,
and the Lion in
"The Wizard of Oz"

D

Age 9

Age 10

Johnny shows his Christmas Card design, before setting off supported by all his friends on the Parish delivery

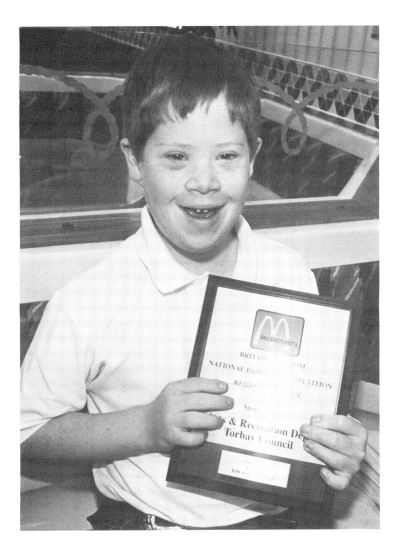

Johnny holding his plaque from "Britain in Bloom"
National Painting Competition

"Hi Mickey I'm having a great time"

The Riding for the Disabled Association developed his natural love and rapport with animals, and gave him confidence and greater physical co-ordination

*Johnny pictured with us on Penny's 16th birthday,
just 6 weeks before he died*

the phone, so there was the contact I felt was right not only for him but also for our benefit, as we did miss him. I continued to be of positive thought and persuasion believing that it was vital that he got used to separation and accepted it as normal. Who knows what the future held for us, and we were getting no younger and there would come a time when we might not be fit enough to care for him at home permanently in the future. As it turned out we are the ones having to come to terms with separation, and it is so difficult. We can identify with the trauma that young mentally handicapped persons must surely endure, when they have of necessity to be parted from their families through illness, old age, or death. It must be so hard, especially if they have never been prepared. The Family Relief Scheme is a gentle way of preparing our special children for personal independence, a development that is natural for the rest of us.

School was of great importance in Johnny's life. He could not get there quickly enough. There was never a day that he did not want to go. Only when he was full of cold, or having a more serious bout of illness, did he stay away. He was picked up in a minibus, and there was always a lady escort to check the children on the journey.

Shirley, then Betty, were two more great loves of his life! He made his mark on these two ladies as he did on everyone with whom he came into contact! Shirley took him through the early school years, and after her retirement Betty took over. Betty had the dubious pleasures of Johnny growing into puberty and all the emotional changes that incurred. He was the ever optimistic suitor for Betty's affections. "Betty's my wife! I'm going out with Betty tonight at 7 o'clock . . . . . going to the pub for a drink. I'm just going upstairs to change," was the never varying line of banter that he greeted me with, the moment he returned from school! It did not matter to Johnny that she was a married lady of many years duration! It's these silly little incidences of fun and laughter that we all miss so much. During the journey to school, about half a dozen youngsters were picked up from various spots in the town, and Johnny led the singing *en route*. What a happy bus load of precious little souls bringing cheer on even the most miserable winter mornings. What Johnny lacked in tune he made up for in enthusiasm. In church his deep gruff voice resounded all around, giving extra special 'umph' to the alleluias; he was always happy when he was singing — what a perpetual source of joy he was.

His school reports were fascinating. From the very early years in the Nursery Class, where he learned basic intellectual skills in word, pattern and number recognition. He related to the content of stories within his own experiences, learnt the signs from the 'Makaton' pre-speech and back-up to early speech development sign language. Music was always a great source of joy, and he took part in a Folk Dance Festival, being a reliable member of the school country dance team. He entered into everything with great gusto! He enjoyed PE, but we always needed to be aware of his heart condition, though in the main Johnny paced himself accordingly. Down's children also have a tendency to a weakness in the vertebrae of the neck, and so I was always anxious when he became more adventurous trying out forward rolls and other gymnastic feats. In the Upper School he took part in the B.A.G.A. award for gymnastics and attained the first levels. He gained confidence in the swimming pool very gradually, and around thirteen years of age he swam without armbands. For years we coaxed and encouraged, but he was very frightened of the water, even when we were in the pool with him. After a course of private lessons, and together with his class lessons in the school hydrotherapy pool and trips to the local Leisure Centre pool, his fear vanished and it was a nightmare trying to get him out!

His reading and writing skills developed slowly over the years. We continued to notice times of great spurts of mental activity and then the times when he seemed to plateau out. He read from a school reading scheme, learning with flash cards of single words, then short sentences, then to a book. Phonics played a part later but his amazing pictorial memory helped him read and retain the words he learnt. He was very keen to do his reading homework and we encouraged him as much as possible. The sense of identifying with his sister doing her homework was a very real need for him. Johnny's speech was an area of considerable concern. He suffered from 'dispraxia' we were told, meaning that the clarity and his inability to pronounce clearly would be severely affected. The signs of the Makaton Scheme helped in the early years. As he became more vocal, speech therapy helped, but it was always to be an area where it was hard and often frustrating for him to speak distinctly. He improvised and mimed and generally made himself understood, but as he got older he was more conscious of it and very frustrated at times. I felt so sad for him as his general knowledge was so wide and his desire to take a full part in any conversation was very keen. We were used to his pronounciation at home and it was easy for us to understand him, but in the wider community it often proved to upset him, and he would stay silent if he was unsure of his environment.

Johnny showed great artistic talent and interest in the creative arts from an early age. The 'Magnadoodle' was one of his favourite mediums for drawing. His lovely childish simplistic interpretations were delightful. His pride knew no bounds when his design was chosen for a Charity Christmas Card in 1991. He was featured in the 'Down's Heart Group' Christmas card having submitted a line of impish robins on the march. The photographs of him, the subsequent write-up in the local press, and the fact that 20,000 cards were purchased and sent out that year added to his self-confidence and esteem. Fame at last! Later on that year he won a plaque and cash prize for a beautiful painting of some buttercups. This was the Britain in Bloom National Painting Competition, sponsored by MacDonalds.

The Saturday morning when we went down town to MacDonalds, began early at home with Johnny rather bemused by the whole idea. "Do I have to?" was his reaction to the urgency of making the appointment in good time. We discussed what was likely to happen during breakfast, and he ate up his two Weetabix (his usual daily breakfast, day in and day out without variation ever since he was a baby) with gusto, after his "mmmm my favourite" as if it was only given as an occasional treat! The scraping of the dish and the gulp of his cup of orange juice preceded his trip to the bathroom. Quite able to wash himself and clean his teeth, he resented the fact that I hovered making sure he paid attention to fine detail this morning. "I know I'll wear my new black jeans" and he agreed that his school T-shirt would be appropriate today as he had entered this competition through school.

Hurrying up the street, he strode out ahead of us, his excitement and sense of importance now very much to the fore. Jon, his headmaster, joined us for the presentation. Now overcome with shyness, the ebullient confident character that strode into MacDonalds, sat passively and nervously by my side. As the children went up for their awards, whispers of "Is it me now?" or "When is my turn?" accompanied each one. "And now in Class 4, in third place is Jonathan Luntz . . . .". A startled jump and "Me now?" He walked confidently up towards the front, chest puffed out, arms swinging to emphasise the somewhat swaggering gait, but shyness returning and cheeks blushed as he accepted his plaque with a polite "Thank you" amid loud applause. A real recognition that he was indeed able to compete and achieve alongside children from all abilities.

We were filled with such pride as we watched the proceedings and I couldn't help but look back and remember the times when I thought his Down's Syndrome would mar his achievements or sense of self-worth, or make him an outcast amongst the rest of us. His role in life was to be more vital than I could have imagined.

School Reports.   Comments -------

Infant Years . . . .

Age 4 — Johnny seems more confident . . . passing through the shy phase of closing his eyes and screwing up his face . . . trying very hard to talk.

4 ¾ — he is looking very healthy and joins in all activities. He babbles constantly and makes his needs known by gesture. Enjoys dressing up in the Wendy House . . . isn't so fussy about getting his hands dirty.

5 — imaginative play very good . . . speech has improved. Johnny is the instigator of play situations . . . drawing becoming more representational.

6 — Integration Programme at Ilsham Primary School a great success.

7 — Needs firm handling . . . has definite ideas about what he wants to do. At present rather boisterous . . . everything seems to end up in a rough and tumble! Johnny is a bright little boy with a lovely happy personality and a good sense of humour. He is a joy to teach.

Lower Junior Years . . . .

Age 8 to 10 — Johnny is making good progress but is sounding me out by using delaying tactics, which will be actively discouraged . . . his behaviour is improving and he now comes in when he is told. Johnny has responded this term and matured. He sets a good example to the younger members of the class. Johnny has made excellent progress and has matured considerably. He is still overcome with embarrassment however, when complimented or praised. I will miss his cheerful smile and leadership next year.

Upper Junior Years . . . .

Age 11 to 12 — Extremely capable at mixing, stirring, spreading and washing-up in Home Economics . . . cooks jacket potatoes, eggs, toast and sandwiches . . . very skilful at dusting, cleaning and vacuuming! Increased confidence in the water, gymnastics and athletics. He has a confident and co-operative attitude to his work and in social situations . . . has an excellent relationship with peers and staff . . . is popular with all . . . making good steady progress.

13 to 14 — Johnny can participate as a speaker and is an attentive listener in group work. His poor articulation makes it difficult to always understand him, though he works hard to make clear what he is trying to say. He has an excellent general knowledge. Johnny is interested in the world around him and takes a very active part in discussions.

Johnny is an extremely pleasant young man who is quick to socialise. Johnny can dress himself and look after his belongings and take care of his personal needs. Johnny can spell many common words and uses a dictionary. He reads well and understands what he has read. Reading Age 7 (Neale Reading Test). He knows simple addition and subtraction and can use a calculator . . . he operates a computer for both mathematical skills and reading and writing. Johnny can now swim 25m of the Clennon Valley Pool . . . he is able to ski on the dry ski slopes but he does need extra encouragement in these activities. He enjoys uni-hoc, PE and the multigym. Johnny is not very enthusiastic when going shopping . . . (because he hates the long walk to get there . . . Mum!) . . . but when he is in the shops he is eager to manage alone . . . he can follow simple picture recipes, but is slow to get on as he is easily distracted. Johnny is always eager and friendly in welcoming visitors and involves them in school activities. He is now using the bus with a college student, to go to his "taster" work experience at the Iceland Frozen Food Centre in town.

*   *   *   *

The extracts from Johnny's School Reports, from age four to almost fifteen, briefly indicate his progress in the many skills to help prepare him for an adult life which would have been full and varied, and with some independence. But it was not to be. Nevertheless the many experiences and opportunities afforded to him made his childhood rich and very fulfilled, and no different to that of any other child of school age. He had the added bonus of weekly visits to our local Primary School, in the neighbourhood integration scheme, where he moved up with his peer group from the age of six to eleven years. It proved a great success not only for Johnny's greater awareness and wider learning situations, but for the 'ordinary' children to befriend him, and observe and cater for his needs. He was welcomed warmly, liked and respected by his friends there. We remain grateful to both heads and staff of each school for their care and the opportunities that they made available for Johnny.

Home life graduated through the usual stages of re-adjustment for me as a mum. The baby and toddler stage, the first taste of freedom without either children when they began playschool albeit for only a couple of hours. The hole that was left when Penny began full-time school, and only a year later both children flown from the nest between 8.30 and 4 p.m. It just wasn't right to be shopping without pushing a pushchair! I missed them dreadfully but blossomed in the forgotten pleasure of knowing myself again. I planned to do so much, but as we all know they were home from school before I could look round.

I always tried to follow my belief in a steady and constant routine; babies and young children need a secure pattern and thrive and respond accordingly. Bedtime did not vary much. Both Penny and Johnny were tired and fell fast asleep by 6.30 p.m., with the time schedule changing as they grew older.

Mike and I needed our evenings together and although it meant early morning awakening, we preferred it this way round, and took turns on the early stint.

We enjoyed some wonderful family holidays. When Johnny was five years old, we decided we could and should not leave him at home, and prepared to risk the possibility of illness abroad. The initial trip of three consecutive years in Menorca, was our first taste of carefully-planned preparations. These consisted of forewarning the airline to be aware of his needs and the possibility of having oxygen to hand; my hand luggage full of antibiotics, laxatives and their opposite number; creams and a letter from our doctor, explaining Johnny's congenital abnormality in his heart in case of any emergency treatment being required in a foreign hospital. Thankfully we did not need to use any of these precautions on any of our holidays. On our first flight with him, as we were taking our place in the baggage queue prior to boarding, I was hugely relieved, and incredibly amazed to see our very own GP and his family in the very same queue; it gave me a wonderful sense of relief. 'We'll be ok now if anything goes wrong.' I don't suppose he felt as thrilled to see one of the patients he was hoping to get away from! Penny was the one to fall victim to chickenpox on our third trip to Menorca. Johnny went down with it on our return, having a wretched time with severe bronchitis to finish it off. Thank God we were in England.

We had several Cornish holidays, one was a wonderful week in a family hotel where the children had exciting events planned for them part of the time, which allowed Mike and I to relax too. A totally new experience in a 'Farm Park' followed; we stayed in a chalet and took Hannah and Simon, Johnny's cousins, with us. They loved the romps in among the bales of hay, the goats and lambs joining us at mealtimes, and the company of lots of playmates.

Our two trips to Florida were the highlights of his life. He was eleven when we went the first time, but was old enough to live the fairy tale of Disney World, Sea World and the other excitements wholeheartedly, to make a lasting impression. A young teenager friend came along with us and she and Penny took the pressure off Mike and I, amusing him when we were exhausted having walked miles around the theme parks pushing Johnny in his buggy. It's a magical place indeed for all the family, and we relived both trips time and time again on our return home, with Johnny recalling every little detail. The magic was stored in his heart and memory for all time. He was sensitive to noise and timid in places like theatres or the cinema. He so wanted to watch the performances, but fear of the unknown took over. Generally he sat face down and his fingers stuffed in his ears! This was the pattern on our first trip, during the amazing shows at Sea World where whales, dolphins and other creatures performed their amazing feats, and no amount of cajolling or persuasion could make him look! I was so annoyed with him. Two years later on our second visit, he had outgrown this phase and we were captivated by his thrills and delight and so relieved that at last he was able to enjoy the events.

On our second trip, when Johnny was nearly fourteen, we included a four-day cruise to the Bahamas. The ship was affiliated to Walt Disney Corporation, so Johnny loved having Mickey, Pluto, Chip and Dale on board, and joined in the delights all day long. The only blight on the horizon was the tropical storm that hit us on our return. Johnny and I spending hours vomiting and moaning together, curled up on a mattress in the children's playhouse, with other youngsters and some of the ship's crew as green around the gills as we were.

Living in Torquay one might imagine us spending all summer on the beach. We rarely did; Johnny was not too interested in sand and sea on the home front. He enjoyed an out-of-season stroll with the dog, throwing pebbles into the water or searching for crabs and shells, wading in the pools in wellie boots, or climbing the rocks, as long as it did not involve a lengthy walk. He never was a great one for a walk. There were times when I found his lack of co-operation on such occasions very trying and restricting. I needed to remind myself constantly of his special needs when patience ran out.

We all enjoyed picnics on Dartmoor. Johnny, although wanting to be with Penny and cousin Sara and friends climbing the Tors, became too breathless if he overexerted himself. We played games of hide-and-seek behind the rocks, and he was happy. The best part of the day out was the food! The never varying choice of ham sandwiches, sausages, crisps, fruit yoghurts with NO bits, and chocolate buttons, afforded us some peace and quiet for a short while. As soon as we had eaten he would be quite happy to return home to his favourite videos and TV programmes. Johnny learnt so much from his videos and TV. It was much more than passive relaxation. He had favourite videos that he played over and over, and it wasn't long before he was able to anticipate what was coming, singing and dancing along with the musical or cartoon comedy, with spot-on accuracy in word and movement. The Nintendo game was a real learning tool for Johnny too. He was able to co-ordinate hand and eye, and he remembered sequences and avoided hazards in the games, with great precision, and soon became as adept as Penny, and beat me every time. The Mario character never got beyond the first obstacle when it was my turn playing against Johnny, much to his disgust . . . "I'll show you Mum . . . .".

We had our own mini zoo in the back garden. A walk-in wire mesh cage was erected by Tom, a builder friend, so that the children could be in close contact with the rabbits, guinea pigs and tortoise. There were multiple births on numerous occasions much to their delight and education, until I decided enough was enough. Our dog during those early years was Polly, an old English sheepdog — an adorably soppy and docile animal, who was inseparable from the children. The animal interaction was a further invaluable learning experience for Johnny. She died at thirteen, and we were heartbroken. Lottie, our present dog, is a chocolate brown standard poodle of considerable intelligence, and devoted to the family. We are a very animal-orientated family, and many of our outings ended up at farm parks, zoos or farms, giving us all pleasure.

There was tremendous loyalty between brother and sister. Often during our evening meal, a heated raised voice would pipe up, "No Mum, Penny right. You wrong Mum" if Penny and I were trying to sort out a difference of opinion. The marked closeness between Johnny and Mike was very evident at all times. He would look up during tea around the fire on a Sunday evening and say "You know what's on tonight Dad.

Last of the Summer Wine. Our favourite.'' Clearing away the dishes I could hear the laughter and feel the complete accord between them.

"Come on Johnny, let's trot.'' Kate encourages the placid shire pony by slapping his side with gusto. Lesley the other helper, (one who was subjected to Johnny's amorous attentions) runs ahead tugging at the leading rein trying to stimulate this docile beast out of its plodding gait. "NO. NO Wait.'' The high-pitched frightened affectation in Johnny's voice fools neither Kate or me, as I watch from the other side of the corral. "Come on chin up, chin up. Are you ready?'' "Oh no not that again! I don't want to trot. No!''
     Argument for argument sake. So typical of Johnny. Just a big tease really. "Steer round the corner. Left hand down on the rein.'' "Do I have to? Yesh! Yesh! Here I go!'' Johnny shouts in glee now as he bobs straight-backed, up and down in the saddle, revelling in the thrill of the action. There is wonderful interaction between child and pony, and skilled commitment from all the volunteers within the Riding for the Disabled Association.

Unbeknown to me, a lot of secrecy surrounded my fiftieth birthday. As I dressed to go out for dinner (just the four of us was what I had requested), I wondered what kind of surprises they had planned for me. Many occasions over the years had seen us at this favourite hotel with its impressive rooms still retaining the splendour of a bygone age, celebrating Christmas when the children were small, or Mother's Day lunches and special birthdays. We had had our wedding reception there and Mike's retirement dinner too. Auntie Jay's eightieth birthday was an elaborate affair with Johnny greeting her with their very own secret code words "Goody-goody gumdrops!'' He and Auntie Jay had a very close and special relationship.
     The crease-resistant silky tunic dress, with the big pearl buttons, was a favourite of Johnny's as it was one where he cuddled up with confidence to his heart's content knowing I wouldn't fuss about a crushed and wrinkled look ensuing. "That's my favourite.'' "Thanks my angel, you look very

smart. Just like Daddy in your navy blazer.'' Johnny beamed
with pleasure and did a quick twirl, with hands in trouser
pockets of course. He loved dressing up for an occasion. He
was also a real smoothy when laying on the compliments
"You look nice Penny. That pink skirt suits you!'' "Thanks
Jon!'' "Dad and me are twins! . . . Come on. Hurry up. I'm
hungry!''

En route for the hotel, we called in at the Church Centre
where Mike worked as the Parish Administrator. His office
was on the lower level of a very modern building adjoining
the church which had been opened in 1986. Penny had played
a big part in the official opening when she, as a young
member of the fellowship at St Matthias, had unlocked the
door into the Centre link. She was nine at the time. "You
wait there love, I won't be a minute, just got to pick up
something,'' Mike said. "Can we come Dad?'' Penny and
Johnny leapt out of the car and followed. And still I didn't
suspect a thing. After calling me inside on some convincing
pretext, I found myself centre stage to a resounding "Happy
Birthday to you'' from fifty family and friends gathered
there. A memorable birthday indeed.

Mike's sixtieth celebration followed two years later and it
was my turn to have the secrets with the children. The party
was again in the very comfortably furnished lounge at the
Church Centre. We were lucky to find an evening when the
room was free, as the bookings are made months and often a
year in advance; it is a place where the whole community is
served and people's needs are met in every way possible, both
spiritually and physically.

Every time I heard "Oh Johnny you're disgusting'' spoken
by his sister, I dreaded to look. There he was filling his plate
with, in the main, sausage rolls and sausages on sticks, piled
high in their dozens. "But I'm hungry Penny.'' With a full
stomach, which is a bit of an understatement, and beginning
to tire, I find him at my side. "When are we going to light the
candles?'' "In a minute love.'' "Can I sing to Dad by
myself?'' "Yes if you think you can. Can you really do it all
by yourself?'' "Yeh. I can.''

There was a deadly hush as Penny lit the candles. All eyes
were on Mike and the cake. Repeated digs in my ribs, and a

persistent whispered "I WANT to sing to my dad." Again a doubtful whisper from me, "Do you really think you can in front of all these people?" A slightly worried look around the room and a glance at his dad. "Yesh." His hand held tightly clasped in mine, with fingernails piercing my skin and his cheeks a little flushed, I manoeuvre him over to his dad, explaining to everyone what was about to happen. Holding both his dad's hands and at first looking down at his boots in embarrassment, he looked up adoringly into Mike's face. A trembling "Happy Birthday to you" became more audible and tunefully confident if somewhat deeper in tone, as he repeated the phrase and completed the verse. There wasn't a dry eye in the house.

Penny's sixteenth was an at-home affair with all the young cousins, her nana and the aunts and uncles, and Penny's friend Dave. Her cake had been made in a local bakers, as my cake decorating skills didn't stretch to a pair of DMs iced into the top! Johnny was in his element with all the youngsters, and on form as usual when we agreed to some party games. He was a scream when playing 'Give Us A Clue' and invented some amazingly realistic mimes to some pretty obscure subjects! His party piece was making an entrance as a male model. "And now everyone a warm round of applause for the famous Jonathan Luntz modelling the latest . . . .". Penny and the teenage scenario had influenced his choice and taste in clothing. The multicoloured and non-matching bootlaces did wonders for his orthopaedic boots, and standing next to his sister in her Doc Martens, he was thrilled to bits.

We needed no excuse to celebrate birthdays in our family; not one passed by without a party over the years. Johnny always managed three parties per one birthday; one for the grandparents, one for the local friends and one in school for his chums, although most years he directed the driver of the school minibus to our house where we normally had a party lunch. I enjoyed making the novelty cakes when he was younger, even if my son flatly refused to eat any of it. He refused to even taste a crumb. It was only in the latter years that he began to eat finger food. Give him sausage and chips any day. He adored the singing, the hurrahs and the blowing out of the candles, which we had to repeat and repeat till the candles burnt out into the icing! His excitement was so infectious, and we got such joy watching him open his cards and presents . . . . "I don't believe it . . . I DON'T believe it . . . I don't BELIEVE it!" The thrill and thanks was the same for a packet of chocolate buttons as it was for a new bike. It taught us a few home truths.

I feel so happy writing these words and being able to share a little of the joys that Johnny brought to us. I'm sure I'll always want to talk to anybody with time to listen. Show me a parent who doesn't want to talk about a beloved child. This child of mine, though no longer with me in a physical sense, lives on through the memories and the love that he brought in such a special way. My life now moves on without his physical presence and I must accept a different direction, but with the lessons learnt from this cherished son, my richly blessed life must grow in even greater strength.

FAITH HOPE AND LOVE

"And what is faith?"

Faith gives substance to our hopes, and makes us certain of realities we do not see.   Hebrews 11 v1. (N.E.B.)

Although the thought of premature death was hanging over my head for most of Johnny's life, nothing could have prepared me for the devastation I felt when it happened.

On Christmas Day evening as Mike and I walked to the car, helping Johnny climb the steps from our house, it just did not enter my mind that he would never be coming back. He was feeling wretched with the pain in his tummy, which was due to an enlarged liver, an indication of heart failure, but he stoically climbed into the back seat of the car. I sat with him cuddled up close to me and reassured him that the doctors and nurses would make him feel better.

The A & E Department luckily did not keep us waiting too long, and after the initial admission we went with him to the ward.

The doctors and nurses were wonderfully kind and caring. It was four days after he had been admitted when the consultant asked to speak privately to Mike and me. Gently she spoke of her fears that he could have Bacterial Endocarditis, as he was not responding to the treatments as quickly as she would have expected. She explained very carefully the nature of this rare disease, and although she stressed recovery was possible, we should be prepared for many weeks of intravenous antibiotics. It was at this moment that a deep feeling inside of me said Johnny's time was near.

Over the next four to five days, when tests proved her suspicions to be correct, I tried to be optimistic. I prayed that he might be spared, and I followed fully all the results of

47

blood and urine tests that were taken regularly day and night. By Saturday it was obvious to me that Johnny's body was not coping and the duty consultant expressed his real concern, and that Johnny was desperately ill. Penny had, only an hour before, arrived back in Torquay having spent New Year with a friend. The shock for her was all-encompassing. We had desperately tried to cling on to hope all week and had not wanted to frighten her over the telephone. Anyhow we ourselves had not been told, until that night, that his chances of recovery now were practically nil. His condition had suddenly deteriorated.

The tensions, the emotional turmoil, and physical exhaustion that accompanied those last few days and nights had me working in overdrive; Johnny's spirit was unbelievable. He was my strength. "I love you Mum" he said so many times during that week. He was happy if I sat on the bed leaning back on the pillow with him; we chatted about favourite things, outings and friends. We coloured in the *Giant Super Fun Book*. We read stories and we sang songs. The words of 'Mary had a baby, Yes Lord' resounded in his room. He sang it to Janyce our deacon, and to Hazel his doctor. He sang at the top of his voice, holding the oxygen mask away from his mouth as if it was a microphone. I was amazed by this burst of exhilarant animation. He asked for sausage and chips for tea. He died the following day.

With his pain eased and controlled we spent every minute of those last twelve hours talking to him, hugging him, telling him how much we loved him, until he fell into a deep sleep and he slowly slipped away.

The actual moment of death for Johnny was peaceful. He simply took two or three deep breaths and sighs and then he lay still.

"Just think . . .
Of stepping on shore and finding it heaven,
Of taking hold of a hand and finding it God's hand.
Of breathing new air and finding it celestial air,
Of feeling invigorated and finding it immortality.
Of passing from storm and tempest
    and finding it unknown calm,
Of waking up and finding it home."

The actual moment of death for me was a racing and pounding of my heart, a numbing of all my senses, heartbreak, but then a feeling of great calm and acceptance.

I cried, I held him, I told him over and over how much I loved him. I looked at him and told myself he was at peace; he looked untroubled and as if he was gently asleep. The several hours we stayed with him after he died were so very precious. In our grief we all held him and we held each other. I felt a remoteness, an unrealness, and as we sorted out his things and prepared to leave, the all-enveloping shock took hold, and protected me during the next few weeks against the pain and reality of his loss that was surely to set in.

Through the times of suffering and pain all along the way of Johnny's life, and at his passing, I can equate to having experienced the heart of God. I have chosen to put my trust in God's will. We all have a free choice. That is Godgiven. My son's creation has been instrumental in influencing the choice I have made; my very special gift of love from God. As a Christian I believe God understands the feelings of bereavement, because the death of Jesus cut off the Father from the son. Intellectually I can never fully understand, nor can I fully know, but by trusting and accepting the faith of the Christian Church I feel an inner peace in God's love and a sure hope for the future. I believe faith is an awakening of the spirit, and in my Christian Faith the Cross has not protected me from the pain, rather it has faced me with it.

During the time between Johnny's passing and his Service of Thanksgiving, I went about the preparations and decision-making and general day-to-day living experiences in a state of unreal control. It was almost as if I was enacting life's scenario outside of my own body. The full impact of my loss and its reality, hit me totally and unexpectedly several weeks afterwards.

I cried no tears at the wonderful Service of Thanksgiving for Johnny's life. I was totally calm and acutely aware of every hymn, prayer and words of the Address. The only time I felt the pain stab was during the last hymn, 'Seek Ye First The Kingdom of God' when I clearly recalled my Johnny singing out the alleluias with such enthusiasm. The service was a triumphant farewell to a boy who had triumphed over all odds. Greeting friends after the service, the short

Committal at the Crematorium, and the gathering at our house of family and close friends, enveloped me in a kind of blanket of composure. The outpouring of compassionate love and care, the prayers that upheld us, over 500 letters and cards that came our way, uplifted our spirits, comforted and strengthened us.

Then the reality struck home. The house is empty of his unique presence. No school bus at 8.30 in the morning, no nagging to hurry with his anorak and not keep Betty waiting. No school bus at 4 in the afternoon, the slamming of doors, the excited laughter and sounds of thumping feet coming down the drive. The jokes with Betty, the daily ritual scolding as he throws his bag on the floor deliberately, then the hysterical shrieks of fun as I chase him upstairs.

The rooms are silent. No noise of the television or the favourite videos of Bugs Bunny cartoons, Laurel and Hardy, to Indiana Jones and James Bond. His bed is empty: no hushed whispering needed after he had gone to bed. No sounds of the clinking and rolling marbles on his tray, the thrilled exclamations when he had achieved another level on his Nintendo games. No fourth place to set at the table; no favourite yoghurts or chocolate buttons to buy. No more sausage and chips. No boy's clothes to wash and iron. His dressing gown hangs unused behind the door, and his collection of teddies, knitted dolls and monkeys, lie unmoved on his bed.

No laughter. No hugs. There is nothing more to do for him. The pain pierces. We are brokenhearted. Will we ever survive this agony?

I seem to be unable to see the features of his darling face as clearly; I can't bear the thought of him being more distant as time passes. I resume the daily routine, but I have no real interest in anything that I am doing; my mind is with Johnny. I begin to feel more cheerful, but should I be feeling this way? It's almost as if I am betraying him by my laughter. But no. Johnny would want me to laugh . . . . I remember how often he said "Be brave Mum . . ." when he sensed things were not quite right. Oh yes. I will be brave. Johnny set such an example. Often I wonder why did he have to die? He seemed to be coping so well and we were optimistic that we would all be together a lot longer. I feel a sense of defeat too. All the years we fought for him and nurtured him, but he had died as a child in spite of all that we had done. I feel cheated. Death has won. I feel closer to death and eternity than to life and worldly things at the moment.

I will myself to accept that what God gives He also takes back. He gave me Johnny — on loan — now He has decided it is time to take him back. I assure myself that even though I cared for him with the whole of my being during his short lifetime, I can be certain that now in God's care he has perfection. I remember the deep emotional experience of his birth. This emotional experience at and after his death is different, yet the same; there is a real sense of being in the presence of something much greater than anything we can know. Our reactions towards untimely death vary from one to another and situation to situation. This is my situation and I am not qualified to understand why. Only God knows. Each life however short or broken, is all part of God's will and His plan for the universe. The Christian message is that death is not the end of life, but just part of the journey and a milestone we all must pass. My son has passed this milestone and his simple trusting faith in the words of Jesus: "I am the resurrection and the life; he who believes in me, though he die, yet shall he live, and whoever lives and believes in me shall never die," ensures his eternal life free from pain.

We need time in our grieving. I write these words just four months after Johnny died. I need time to live alongside my grief. I need to hold all the memories happy and sad, close to me. I need understanding and love from my nearest and dearest ones. Mike and Penny need this. Mike needs time. Penny needs time. We grieve separately. We must channel our love for one another to a closer but more open understanding, where no points of inner pain and conflict are left unspoken if we are to survive. In all this human agony we cling on to the hope of God's promises in Jesus Christ. In a biblical sense I wonder is this the pain that Christ felt when He died, and is the separation that God the Father felt on the first Good Friday, what we are feeling? We cling to these promises of new life declared on that first Easter Day. Believing in faith we can be at peace in the knowledge that our beloved Johnny is whole in that eternal life — heaven — the like of which I cannot know, it being totally outside my earthly experience, except that it is glory, beauty and peace, and love, if our God is the God of love we believe Him to be. A loving God made us all in His own image to reflect Himself. Love shows us that God exists. Johnny brought God's love to us so forcefully that our lives can never be quite the same again. We have been permanently enriched and humbled. The gift that Johnny brought and the legacy that he has left is LOVE. The words of the song say it all . . . "Love changes everything".

I am reminded also of the very well-known passage in the Bible from St Paul's letter to the Corinthians in the New Testament. It shows us the best way for us to use our very own Godgiven individual talents and differing abilities. It shows me that Johnny's inbuilt loving nature truly reflects the image that God would wish us all to be.

"If I speak in the tongues of men and of angels, but have not love, I am only a resounding gong or a clanging cymbal. If I have the gift of prophesy and can fathom all mysteries and all knowledge and if I have a faith that can move mountains, but have not love, I am nothing. If I give all I possess to the poor and surrender my body to the flames, but have not love, I gain nothing.

Love is patient, love is kind. It does not envy, it does not boast, it is not proud. It is not rude, it is not self-seeking, it is not easily angered, it keeps no record of wrongs. Love does not delight in evil but rejoices in truth. It always protects, always trusts, always hopes, always perseveres.

Love never fails. But where there are prophecies they will cease; where there are tongues they will be stilled; where there is knowledge, it will pass away. For we know in part, and we prophesy in part, but when perfection comes, the imperfect disappears. When I was a child. I talked like a child, I thought like a child, I reasoned like a child. When I became a man, I put childish ways behind me. Now we see but a poor reflection as in a mirror; then we shall see face to face.

Now I know in part; then I shall know fully, even as I am fully known.

And now these three remain: faith, hope and love. But the greatest of these is love.''

So now I treasure the memories in my heart of that floppy rag doll-like baby, with his chubby hands, squat fingers, cherub lips, bent over ears and sandy red hair. The potbellied toddler, his legs disproportionally short for the length of his body. The little freckled-nosed uniformed schoolboy, proudly trundling off with his school bag almost as big as himself over his arm. The growing adolescent with his hair more fair than red, the changing shape of his body with its muscular shoulders and his voice now gruff in its manly image. Oh how I love him so. And through these ever-changing scenes of life's growth, that wonderful smile and laughter, and the unconditional love that shone from his grey-blue eyes with such intensity, will lift my spirit forever.

THE ADDRESS

The Reverend Janyce Pringle
Service of Thanksgiving for the life of Jonathan Luntz
January 12th 1993

Your presence here today says more than words can ever tell about the magnetism of one small boy, whose life among us was short, but as someone in this congregation said 'He managed to give more love in his fifteen years, than some of us will manage in a lifetime.' Johnny, as Jill so touchingly describes it, came in an unexpected and different wrapping, but Mike and Jill called their baby 'Jonathan' a gift from God. A perfect name for Johnny Luntz.

Just a week before Christmas, I preached a sermon here about Mary who was found to have favour with God, and she was chosen to bear his son Jesus; and as Mary watched over her son from Bethlehem to Calvary, did she ever wonder that the favour from God was only an illusion? A Christian knows that often it is in hardship, in pain, in bewilderment, in suffering, in loss that we experience God in much greater depth. And when we confront such hardship in company with God, we grow and deepen in faith. It is lives that have been given something great to do and even to bear, although they may have been bruised in the process, that truly know the favour of God, and this favour rested on Mike and Jill and Penny.

Johnny was a very special boy, but he was born into an equally special family. Honed by pain and concern for Johnny's health over the years, but wonderfully rich and vibrant and alive with so much love and laughter and kindness and understanding. Everyone who knew Johnny loved him. There was no unkindness, no malice, no hate, no spitefulness in Johnny. He had a terrific sense of humour and

54

he could see jokes you didn't expect him to understand. He had an amazing memory, he never forgot things he was told. He was a very gregarious child, he really loved people old and young, and adored little babies with whom he was very gentle. He loved being included with Penny and her friends, and his best mate was Mike, with whom he had a wonderful rapport. Those of us who were at Mike's birthday party last year, will never forget Johnny singing 'Happy Birthday' to his dad. It was an unforgettable and moving occasion.

A year ago this Christmas, Johnny designed the winning card for the Down's Heart Group Competition, and it was a particular joy for us at St Matthias as we chose Johnny's card to be our Church Christmas Card, and 3,000 of them were delivered, one to every home in the Parish.

Jill spoke so beautifully through the *Herald Express* saying that the love and beauty that shone from Johnny was God Himself showing through. As I spoke with a friend the other evening telling him about Johnny, the friend observed 'He's changed your life hasn't he?' And during the twelve days that Johnny was in hospital it was a privilege to minister to Johnny and his family, but Johnny administered to me. And on the night before he died and I put my hand on his head and said 'Goodnight and God Bless', he reached for my hand, and took it and put his other hand on top so that my hand was clasped between his, and he asked God to bless me, and our prayer together was utterly moving. But another aspect of Johnny's illness that is unforgettable was the trust, the trust that he showed. He bore without murmur the drips, the syringes, the oxygen mask. He was full of courage and full of faith. He never showed fear. When he found speaking difficult his eyes continued to show the trust, and I was reminded of the words of Jesus, 'Unless you become like children you will never enter the kingdom of heaven.' Johnny was and is a true child of God.

I recall seeing many times J. M. Barrie's wonderful play 'Peter Pan'. The story of the boy with perpetual youth. There is a scene where Peter has been confronted and wounded by his arch enemy Captain Hook, and is left alone on a solitary rock in the middle of a great lagoon. The water rises and as the curtain falls at the end of the scene Peter Pan cries out,

'To die will be a very great adventure.' A boy's words, a Christian's faith.

John Dunkerley, Johnny's headmaster at Mayfield School, has said of Johnny's death, 'A light has gone out in our school,' and all our lives are diminished by Johnny's passing, but we are all enriched and changed by having known and loved him. As we give thanks to God for all that Johnny 'the bright star' was and still is, let us commend him to the love and mercy of God, remembering with thankfulness that death is not the extinguishing of the light, but the putting out of the lamp because the dawn has come.

TRIBUTES

These are just a few of the 550 and more tributes that we received after Johnny died, that say it all:—

Johnny is and was about love . . . it is a privilege to have known him and felt his love so freely given . . . .

I will always remember Johnny as a fun-loving person, someone who would always cheer you up if you were down, and always had a smile on his face . . . .

He was unique . . . he radiated happiness and a little of it always rubbed off on contact . . . you were truly fortunate to have had him . . . .

We will never forget Johnny. He only had a short life, but was such an inspiration to us all. He gave out such innocent love and trust. We felt he was a special child of God . . . .

Johnny asked for little but gave so much . . . .

The world is a better place for having people like Johnny in it . . . .

He has probably affected more lives than you will ever realise . . . .

. . . . your son, a treasure indeed for Jesus . . . .

Dear Johnny — his cheerful sunny presence will be sadly missed . . . I remember him always holding up his smiling face for a kiss . . . .

. . . . the love that radiated from Johnny was an example of what true unashamed perfect love is all about. If only the rest of us loved each other the way Johnny did . . . .

He was a shining light of enveloping warmth . . . .

He was a real treasure with so much for us all to learn . . . .

Johnny's gift to me was that he taught me more about myself than he ever knew . . . he was a blessing to so many . . . .

We will remember him as a kind and caring young man . . . for many years he made my days so much brighter and gave me so many laughs . . . .

Johnny made our lives so full lively and at times very wet . . . . (swimming teacher)

We both feel very honoured to have met him, and to have helped look after him . . . .

Johnny was like a little beacon . . . he achieved more in his life than many do in three score years and ten . . . .

He was a star and his light shines on . . . .

Not many people can leave this life leaving such memories behind them . . . .

It's a paradox that where there is so much love there is also the pain; it is reassuring to know Johnny's love and joy continue here but are now glorified in another dimension as well . . . .

EPILOGUE

In the evening of the first anniversary of my son's death, I find myself sitting in the Odeon Cinema watching Walt Disney's film 'Aladdin'. Mike, Penny and I filled our day busily. She, supported by two loyal school friends, and we enjoying a drive on a sunny January afternoon. Each with our own thoughts about this time last year; the pain surfacing more intensely again now, but knowing in our hearts that Johnny would have fully approved our choice of film. 'Aladdin', the fairy tale of magic, adventure, good triumphing over evil, and love winning through in the end.

Throughout this first year apart from Johnny in a physical sense, though united with him in our hearts, we have started out along the bereavement pathway. For me the bereavement pathway that has run parallel to the road of faith, has helped provide the strengthening link to get me through. There has been no flash of lightning or miraculous overnight release of pain, but the road to Calvary and the Cross has challenged me to see myself as I really am in this my situation. In my weak and vulnerable moments, I have found myself shouting out 'Where are you God?' but by hanging in there, and clinging to the Grace of God,

Great
Riches
At
Christ's
Expense

I have discovered Him very close. I have learnt that although the initial denial of acceptance of the death of a dearly loved one is normal, if prolonged leads only to a despair that sees no hope and no triumph. For me, all along the way of Johnny's birth and life, negative thoughts and responses were gradually transformed into positive ones. It is beginning to be so with his death.

> I shall no longer run from sorrow
> nor seek to avoid him
> by going down another street of thoughts.
> I shall not try to overcome him with my strength
> I shall open the door of my heart to his knock
> and let him come in
> whether he be sorrow for my own loss
> or for the world's pain.
> I will learn to live with him steadfast and tender
> and someday the child, Happiness,
> will play in the sunshine
> on the floor of my house.

I am greatly encouraged as I go to my son's school now, when I see the very special 'Light Room' that has been created in his memory. To the many many friends who so generously donated money, we are grateful. The once bare and sparsely-furnished treatment room has been transformed into an area of both peace and calm, whilst at the same time there is a myriad of colour and brilliance from the special fibre optics that have been fitted there. These amazing inventions of the new technology create pulsing fine lights that change from one colour to another, illuminated bubbles floating in a floor to ceiling tube, something resembling a massed brilliance of coiled string, that can be handled safely by the dear little children that have such extra special needs. These lights offer both a mental stimulation and a mental and physical calming sensation. The room is in constant use. Nothing could have been more appropriate. Johnny 'the bright star' or 'the shining light' as he was described in a newspaper article. His radiance shines on his school, helping his playmates to find a level of happiness, within the peaceful tranquillity of this room. Light is a symbol used in all the great faiths, and in the

Christian Faith, Jesus is the light above all lights — God's own son whose light can lift the darkest area in one's life.

Although my Christian faith continues to strengthen me, equally so I have needed to know and feel the love of my family and friends. The care shown by friends who do or do not share my spiritual beliefs has been heartwarming. To feel the genuine warmth of human nature has been a huge support system. I have opened my soul on so many occasions and I thank those who have listened. They have helped in more ways than they could possibly ever realise, simply by being there with an ear, a kind word, or a grasp of an arm. Isn't this after all the loving nature of God shining through the good of humanity? I'm so thankful in knowing the joy that can come from worshipping this good and loving God, through His Son Jesus in a living faith.

The Compassionate Friends are an International Organisation of bereaved parents, offering friendship and understanding to other bereaved parents, and they have much literature. Much of the information is in simple leaflet form geared to individual family member's needs. There are also newsletters whereby one can send in and receive any relevant correspondence. The Compassionate Friends say there is no membership fee, for we have paid the ultimate price in having lost our child.

The Down's Heart Group has played an important part too throughout Johnny's life, and now after his death. Conversations on the telephone with other Mums who have experienced the same loss, have brought a closeness and a bond of love, even though we are complete strangers. All these links have been of immense benefit, their care and concern helping me down this pathway, a pathway that is particularly difficult and painful since the natural order of things has gone awry.

Membership of the Down's Syndrome Association, joining in the local group meetings, the regular newsletters, the meetings held in various locations throughout the country, bringing us all close, has encouraged, educated, and strengthened us over the years. These self-help and support groups act as a buttress, a mind of information, a source of great comfort and stand as a testament to the love shown by human beings one to another.

Although I like to think of Johnny's life as a life differently abled NOT disabled, and one completed, as he had had an exuberance for living and had not wasted a moment of his fifteen years, I think the following verse sums up all my feelings as I bring my story to a close:

"We cannot judge a biography by its length or by the number of pages in it; we must judge by the richness of the contents . . . . sometimes the 'unfinished' are among the most beautiful symphonies."

And so now I am remembering my very own 'unfinished' symphony that will remain the most beautiful for evermore.